THE EFFORTLESS

Empire

The time-poor professional's guide
to building wealth from property

THE EFFORTLESS
Empire

The time-poor professional's guide
to building wealth from property

CHRIS GRAY

Published in Australia by:

Go For Your Life Pty Ltd

Level 14, 309 Kent Street, Sydney NSW 2000

PO Box N64, Grosvenor Place NSW 1220

Phone: 02 9994 8944

www.yourempire.com.au

A CIP catalogue record for this book is available from the National Library of Australia.

ISBN: 978-0-646-49326-8

Designed by Andy Pilkington

Typeset by The Messenger Group

Printed in China through Messenger Print Brokerage

Project managed by The Messenger Group

www.themessengergroup.com.au

Acknowledgements

My main thanks for helping me to produce this latest book is to the property market. If it wasn't for you I would never have created the freedom and choice that has given me the time to write it. You've also given me the financial freedom to hire great professionals to assist in producing a much better book than I could have alone.

My thanks also goes out to Lowell Tarling, who, once again has helped me turn my spoken words into something I am proud to put on the bookshelf. Together I hope we change many other people's lives for the better.

Thanks to my gorgeous wife Tanya for supporting me and bringing Scott (and his yet to be born sister) into our lives.

Andy Pilkington and Nick Richardson thanks for your creative help with the new vision for the business. Tiffany Logan, well done for giving up the 9–5 and partnering me on the other side.

Mum, after all those bad school reports, who would have believed I've written yet another book!

As a team you've helped me do a great job.

Enjoy the read…

Contents

Foreword

This is a great opportunity for all Australians to learn the secrets of the smartest people in property over many years. Chris has an amazing ability to articulate in an easy to understand way the essential guidelines that are required to create wealth through property. This is must read for people of all generations, backgrounds and income levels interested in property in a secure and tested environment for solid investment returns. Having watched Chris's work for many years and indeed his ability to follow his own advice I suggest that the information contained herein will be both informative and leading edge.

Anthony Bell
CEO of award winning accounting and advisory firm Bell Partners

Introduction

Money gives you choices. The more money you have, the more freedom you generally have. Whether you choose to spend your money on material possessions, use it to spend more time with your family or give it away to charitable causes, would you like to learn how you can generate more from your current income and time?

If you're a high income earner ($100k +) you're likely to have a different wealth creation strategy than middle and lower range earners. After interviewing more than a thousand high income earners I discovered that a high income doesn't guarantee you'll be wealthy or happy. What counts is what you do with it.

The Effortless Empire explains how you can use your high income to create more passive wealth to a point where you could even completely replace your current income. The ultimate aim is to give you more freedom and choice so that you can decide whether you want to continue working or not. After making successful investments, many readers may choose to continue their lives as before; others might work less or they may move into a different field.

While others create a high level of wealth and passive income through business or shares, I have achieved the same goals from investing in property. The choice is yours, but before you make it please understand the true pros and cons of each. Making a decision based on dinner party conversations or newspaper reports which are targeted to the masses is not how you should make an informed decision.

As a high income earner I'm assuming you are already busy enough, so this book is meant as an executive overview similar to one you might receive in a board meeting.

At the end of each chapter of *The Effortless Empire* I have added what I'm calling a Reality Check.

This consists of a few basic questions that test your financial beliefs and attitudes to money. The questions relate to the information in the preceding chapter and are prompts to view what I've just said from your personal perspective. Remember everyone is different and the path I'm advocating in this book is not a path that everyone will take. But as you read each Reality Check, if you find yourself answering 'yes' to many of the questions, then you're the sort of person who can benefit from my approach.

By the end of *The Effortless Empire* you will have discovered:

- *that a high income doesn't make you wealthy, it's what you do with it that counts*

- *as well as making the most of your income, the unused equity in your own home is often the key to making serious wealth in a fraction of the time*

- *property can be a great way to build wealth as it leverages your time, leverages your money, it's passive and it's solid bricks and mortar*

- *how to build a property investing strategy that gives you the keys to minimising your risk*

- *how to make rational financial decisions rather than emotional ones*

- *how to make your property self-sustaining so you won't need to fund it from your limited wages*

- *how and why you need to build a professional team of advisers to implement your strategy*

- *how you can build a large property portfolio without having to sacrifice any of your current lifestyle*

- *the real truth about debt and whether or not it is a good or bad thing,*

- ***and most of all***, *why property only has to grow at 3–4% pa in the long term for you to make money.*

About the author

My name is Chris Gray and I'm the host of Your Property Empire on Sky News Business channel. I started investing at the age of 22 with $35k. Nine years later at 31 I'd turned it into a $3.5 million portfolio and retired from full-time work. Six years after that I've now tripled that portfolio to well over $10m and it still takes me less than a couple of hours a month to oversee it.

Until recently I've never earned more than a $100k salary so if you earn more than that just imagine how big a portfolio you could create. Over more than a decade of buying property, I've never sold any of my real estate; I've still got everything I've ever bought. The reason is because I'm buying investments that are good for the next 30+ years.

Many of my family, friends and work colleagues began asking me how I did it and so I started teaching them the steps I had taken. Over the last six years I've taught thousands of people in big seminars, small groups and individually. My clients have ranged from 15 year old high school kids to middle income earners, all the way to very wealthy business people. I've taught hundreds of accountants, real estate agents, mortgage brokers and bankers how to understand property better and how they in turn can help their clients.

I have found that many of my clients want to copy exactly what I have done but they work very long hours, so half my time is now spent building property portfolios for time-poor professionals who have the income and equity to build real wealth but they don't have the time, knowledge or contacts to put it into practice.

The other half of my time is spent with my newborn son Scott. It's called a balanced life which is possible for me solely as a result of investing in property.

If you would like the freedom to make similar choices in your life, then please enjoy my book. I invite you to let me help you turn your investment aspirations into reality.

1

You're on a good salary. So how come you're not getting rich?

1

Even if you're well paid, salary income alone is unlikely to make you rich. I observed this before my property investments gave me the freedom I now enjoy, back in the days when I had a regular 'job'.

Eureka!

As an accountant and recruitment manager at Deloitte Touche Tohmatsu in Sydney, Australia, it was my job to interview Financial Controllers and Chief Financial Officers (CFOs) who typically earned six-figure salaries and I interviewed over 1,000 of them. Being young I initially thought, 'On $100k+ per annum these people must be rich! They surely must be able to do whatever they want with their lives!'

However, the more executives I interviewed, the more I could see that, behind the veil, these people weren't as wealthy as you might think. Their tax bill alone halved that big salary. And most of their remaining income was spent on improved living standards.

The reality of earning a $100k+ pa income often required their working 60 hours a week, and to do that doesn't leave room for much else – like family or leisure time. So they were neither wealthy financially nor time-wise.

So after being initially impressed, I came to realise that sure, these people lived in bigger houses, drove better cars, enjoyed better holidays, ate in better restaurants, but they were not necessarily building freedom and choice for later life. They weren't building the assets that would make them wealthier when they eventually did give up work. These people were in a similar position as those earning less money. Yet they were committed to full-time work, trading their time for money.

As I interviewed more and more of these executives, I realised I had to do something different otherwise the same truths would eventually apply to me, no matter how often I was promoted.

Some people end up worse off

I thought, 'What's the point of doubling your salary if it doesn't make you wealthier? Maybe you don't automatically get rich on your salary alone'. This was the impression that played on my mind. As I kept on interviewing, every day I continued to be confronted with the same abject lesson: *having a big income doesn't actually make you richer, often you just get bigger debts.*

In fact, because of their increased spending habits, some of these people ended up deeper in debt because their borrowing capacity had gone up and they were still on their credit limits. As a high income earner there is peer group pressure and society expectations that you live in a nicer area, drive a nicer car, send your kids to the 'right' school, etc, etc. They found themselves in a spiralling financial circle. That is, spiralling down.

Building a better tomorrow starts today

And then comes the bad news: if you're on a $200k–$300k pa job and in your late 40s or early 50s, with a new generation hot on your tail, there's a chance that your high salary may not last forever. The recruitment industry taught me that business life is volatile and with restructures, redundancies, takeovers and collapses, no one is irreplaceable. And it may not be easy to get an equally high paying job.

What if everything does change and you do find yourself retrenched with all the expenses of your $200k–$300k job tailgating you? This is even tougher on people on $500k–$750k pa. It might take them 2–3 years to get another job at that level, *if they ever get one!* I'm not trying to depress anyone but it's better to know your actual financial standing so that you can plan ahead and do something about it.

One day, the Deloitte division that I was part of faced a possible closure, which got me thinking outside the square. And rather than jumping into the next job straight away, I thought why not take the opportunity to enjoy an extended holiday? Once you're on the career ladder, extended breaks rarely become a reality. Better to celebrate being out of work with time on your hands than to regret it! And that gave me the time to review the world around me and to catch my bearings.

From my observations I learned – yes – having a higher income does make it easier to invest but unless people put the time and effort into doing it now nothing will change in their future. With hindsight, a lot of people come to realise this after they've spent 20–30 years on a career path, and then it's too late to make the most of leveraging their high salary.

Building a better tomorrow starts today. It's like saying in six months time you plan to run a marathon, yet today you are 10kg overweight and you don't exercise. Unless you set the goal and plan towards it by combining good diet and exercise, do you really think you will run a marathon in six months – or ever? Nothing changes if nothing changes. Failing to set your financial goals and make the necessary adjustments means that the best you can honestly hope for is the same that you already have; a commitment to a job and a boss, and a time-poor lifestyle.

To live in a big house, put the kids through school and go on overseas holidays requires a lot more money than it seems. Let's look at the simple numbers:

- *$300k pa strips back to $150k after tax*

- *at 8%–9% interest, someone with a $1 million mortgage is paying almost $100k pa in interest repayments to keep the house*

- *this only leaves $50k for everything else.*

To make the numbers simple tax is assumed at 50% throughout this book.

Are you too busy earning a salary to build real wealth?

The other common characteristic that I observed among high income earners was that their work environment was so pressured that it often didn't allow them to spend time organising their personal investments because they needed all their limited outside-work hours to enjoy what was left of their family life. The majority of employees and business owners are simply too busy with their day-to-day lives to spend any time managing their personal wealth.

Wouldn't you prefer to choose to work?

Have you stopped to consider whether you are living the lifestyle you want? If you had a $1–$2 million windfall – would you continue working? While some people might retire, the majority might continue in the same job but wouldn't work those long hours. As the pressure would be off they could just enjoy the personal development and social aspects of their job, which has its appeal.

For most of us, windfalls don't really come round, so it makes sense to use your high income to underpin guaranteed wealth for later life.

Summary

After observing over a thousand high income professionals, I have discovered that even if you're well paid, salary income alone isn't enough. If you want to make yourself rich from a time and money perspective, you've really got to do something cleverer than most.

- *As your salary increases, so does your standard of living. You're invariably spending more than you're earning. If you're earning $200k rather than $100k – instead of being $10k in credit card debt (like those on modest salaries) you're probably down $20k–$30k.*

- *If you've got a 50–60 hour a week job, you probably don't have time to concentrate on making personal investments. Maybe you are one of those people who keeps hoping that next year you'll get a $50k bonus and become even richer. Even if those hopes do come true, you still won't have the time to carefully invest, so your $25k after tax will simply disappear along with the rest of your earnings.*

- *And even with those bonuses, if you manage to put aside $100k every year for 10 years (which most people never do) you will only have saved $1 million. True, $1 million is a lot to the average person but if you want to be really wealthy $1 million in 10 years' time isn't much.*

- *If you spent less than you earn, have you been investing those savings in the best possible manner? Paying down your mortgage is one strategy, but are there bigger and better opportunities that you haven't had time to consider?*

- *If you stopped work tomorrow what passive income would you receive from your investments and would that enable you to live the life you really want?*

Most people have never been educated in the area of personal finances and so while they over-achieve at work, they often don't achieve the same level of success in managing their personal wealth. We spend years in educational institutions learning how to earn a high salary, but we don't even spend one week learning how to invest it to maximum advantage.

The good news is, being a high income earner, even if you are time-poor, there are plenty of things you can do. And they may not be the things you have previously discussed with your financial planner or accountant.

REALITY CHECK

Do you work more hours than you would choose to?

◯ Yes   ◯ No

Do you wish you had more time to spend with family and friends?

◯ Yes   ◯ No

Do you have hobbies and leisure interests you would like to devote more time to?

◯ Yes   ◯ No

Do you feel your work schedule compromises your health and fitness?

◯ Yes   ◯ No

Did you expect to feel 'better off' by this stage of your life?

◯ Yes   ◯ No

Are you sometimes apprehensive about your ability to maintain your lifestyle in retirement?

◯ Yes   ◯ No

If you've answered 'yes' to any of these questions, keep reading.

2

It's not about how much you earn, it's what you do with it that counts

2

Being a high salary earner you may not realise how lucky you really are – you're probably in the top 1%–2% of income earners in the country and you've got everything you need to propel you into the next stage of affluence, the only thing you might need now is the mindset.

Most people think you get rich by either making more money (from working) or saving more money, but being a high income earner puts you in the fortunate position where you can place your money more cleverly to get a better result than 90% of the community.

Concentrate on increasing assets

Rather than surmise, 'How can I earn more income?' think, *'How can I acquire more appreciating assets which are going to replace my income?'* This way all your eggs are not in one basket. If you lose your job, you'll still have your investments.

Your salary is limited by your hours

For most people, their salary is always going to be limited by their available time and there are only 24 hours in their day. But there's always a ceiling on it, no matter how much you earn per hour, whereas there is no ceiling on investment profits. Whether you control five or 10 properties or $1 million or $5 million in shares, with help you can manage the whole portfolio in just a few hours per week. And, of course, as you make more money the cycle keeps regenerating itself.

Equity can be your catalyst even if you don't have the income

We've all been brought up to pay down our mortgages as quickly as possible because our parents' generation taught us that 'debt isn't a good thing' and 'you need to own your own home'. But times have changed. Debt can be a good thing if it's used wisely to buy appreciating assets. After people have paid off their own home, they are frequently hit by the realisation that they have missed other opportunities. Indeed, they haven't even considered them!

If you are a high income earner with large amounts of equity you are sitting on a gold mine of potential wealth creation. It's just a case of understanding what that opportunity is and realising the associated risk.

Debt can be advantageous

My parents' generation believed they'd get rich by saving their money – look after the pennies and the pennies will look after the pounds. Today debt is now often seen as good economic management. For example, debt can be used to purchase twice as many appreciating assets thus enabling you to make twice as much money. On one hand, paying off your home loan reduces your non-deductible debt; on the other, using that equity to leverage yourself into more assets will make you considerably more than you could save.

Paying $100k off your home loan might save you $8,000–$9,000 of interest, whereas investing $100k into a $500k property might make you $40k–$50k per year. It's all about focusing on the big picture.

You needn't sacrifice your lifestyle

Many people don't invest in assets because they don't want to sacrifice their current lifestyle. Given the choice between (a) lying on a white sandy beach in Thailand after a long lunch of fresh seafood or (b) not going on holiday and putting all spare cash into investments – most people would rather go on holiday.

I believe you can have both. And to do so you don't have to sacrifice your current lifestyle. I believe you can develop a strategy where you can have more lifestyle now and more wealth later on.

The secret is in understanding the numbers and changing your mindset.

You don't need to be an expert

You don't need to be an expert nor do you need specialist knowledge to build a wealth creation strategy, you just need to know who to go to for advice. When it comes to implementing that strategy, there are managed fund experts who will have more company information than you would ever know, and there are property experts that will have the inside track on what, where and when to buy. The key mindset is in learning to outsource rather than thinking you've got to do it all yourself.

Each of us is an expert in our business roles. Therefore you need to acknowledge your own expertise and the expertise of others in different fields. Don't be afraid to pay for professional services. The success of your investment begins here. If you have a toothache, do you fix it yourself or do you go to the dentist? Do you service your own car or take it to the dealership/mechanic? What about at tax time, do you complete your own tax return or take it to your accountant? While some of you may in fact attempt to do some of these services yourself (hopefully not the dental work), do you not think you'd get more tax deductions if you used an accountant rather than doing it yourself? Think about what you do everyday in your role – if I were to come along and try to do what you do everyday how successful would I be? Would it take me longer to do your job? Would I do the job as well as you? Could I even do your job at all?

Surrounding yourself with a team of qualified professionals is undoubtedly the second-best investment you can make. The best investment you can make is property.

A long term wealth-creating strategy takes time

Creating a long term wealth strategy takes time. The idea is to buy safe, solid assets that will go up in value if you hold onto them for 10, 20, 30 years. You should take as many steps as possible to identify all the potential risks and then put insurances in place so that all of those risks are minimised. You've worked hard to earn your income, so make the most of it!

REALITY CHECK

Is your income earning ability limited by your skills, experience and time?

☐ Yes ☐ No

Are you currently in the process of paying off your home?

☐ Yes ☐ No

If so, has your home risen in value since you bought it?

☐ Yes ☐ No

Are you prepared to take a long term view of your wealth creation plan?

☐ Yes ☐ No

If you've answered 'yes' to any of these questions, keep reading.

3

Why property is such a good way to build and hold wealth

There are generally three main ways through which to achieve real wealth in today's world:

1. Business

2. Shares

3. Property

Each has its pros and cons. In an ideal world you'd have a balance of all three, plus some cash on hand to ensure you can meet your short term commitments.

Let's take a high level overview of each from a personal investment perspective so we can see which might give you the best opportunity to make the most of your income with your limited time.

Business

Owning a business can be a great way to build wealth, a benefit that you generally reap when you sell. The more profitable you can make it and the more you can systematise it, the greater the chance of increasing your sale price.

If you currently own your own business, you may want to have a wealth creation strategy that is diversified into something else so that all your eggs are not in one basket.

If you're a high income earner working for someone else you may find it hard to find the time to set up a part-time business as an additional investment.

Some of the key issues to consider include:

- *Owning your own business is hard work – and even when you're not working in the business you will find yourself thinking about it after hours. It often takes many years to establish and statistically 80% of small businesses go bust in their first five years.*

- *There are often a lot of fixed overheads and set-up costs, including premises, fixtures and staff. These overheads are often payable day and night whether the business is open or not. This usually involves a huge upfront investment and ongoing working capital injections.*

- *If you take on staff you often end up spending more time managing them than you do managing the enterprise.*

- *Most people are already too busy with their own careers without having the time to set up a part–time business, so doing it properly is really left to those who can do it full-time.*

- *It's important to systematise the business so that it is not dependent on you, otherwise it won't be saleable.*

- *It's also important to have an exit strategy otherwise owning a business can be more demanding than having a job.*

Shares

Share trading is one of the classic ways of investment as you can start with almost any amount of money and they can be traded on the stock exchange.

Some of the things to consider are:

- *Shares are a liquid asset and can be easily sold.*

- *There is an element of skill when picking shares as not all rise over time. It takes valuable time and knowledge to develop that expertise.*

- *You can outsource the management of your portfolio to a fund manager or stockbroker. You need to find someone with whom you feel comfortable who will call you ahead of other clients if you need to get in or out of something quickly.*

- *You can normally leverage your money with shares. Blue chip shares can often be leveraged by 50%–80% but other shares may not be possible to leverage at all.*

- *A major downside of leveraging money into shares is the danger of margin calls. Margin calls have brought down many a millionaire. Many share investors have been caught by a dip in the market and been put into a forced sale position. Limiting your gearing to 50% and only choosing blue chip stocks will reduce your exposure.*

- *Share investing can be volatile and no matter how good a company is, if the market falls, nearly everything falls with it. The majority of the nation's superannuation funds have typically been placed in the share market and following a crash many 65 year olds have found they can't afford to retire as planned.*

- *Shares can sometimes be worth nothing: **zilch**.*

Property

Property is often seen as an easy-to-understand investment as we all live in one and therefore we all have a reasonable knowledge of what is good real estate and what is not.

A quick snapshot of investing in property would include:

- *Well chosen residential property is almost guaranteed to rise in the long term because of the basic fact that land is in short supply and our population is increasing.*

- *Getting into property requires a much larger investment (deposit) than shares. The entry and exit costs are significantly higher too.*

- *Property gives you more leverage than most other investments as banks often lend 80%–100% of its value.*

- *Tenancy and maintenance issues can put off many investors, however these can be outsourced to a property manager.*

- *Property is often seen as not being very liquid but that is not necessarily the case. As your property grows, so does your equity and it's very simple these days to have redraw accounts to access that equity. More about that later.*

- *Property will never be worth nothing – it's solid bricks and mortar, and land.*

How the rich people get rich

If you want to learn how to get rich, why not do what the rich people do?

What do the rich people do? If you read the annual *BRW Rich List* you will see that every year around 70%–80% of people on that list have either predominantly made their money through property or they hold their money in property.

I've been investing in property since the age of 22 and over that time I've read many real estate books, attended seminars, learned from property experts and been involved in many discussions about the pros and cons of different strategies. Over the years I have invested lots of time and money trying to get the total picture. My pure focus was about how to make more money from property.

I now understand that:

- *Higher income people have a different mindset and play by different rules to those who are less successful.*

- *There are many misconceptions about investing that really are not true, or at least are not significant when you have a high income (for example, positive cash flow versus negative gearing).*

- *Being a specialist in an investment area often means that you can reap higher rewards than average investors.*

For me, property investing started off simply as home ownership, but as time has gone on I now see it as a solid basis for any wealth creation strategy. I'd like to detail its benefits and how to get over the issues that may have stopped you moving into property in the past.

This could be the vehicle that builds you enough wealth to free up your life.

Easy to understand

Sometimes the best laid plans are the simplest and when it comes to investing in property, residential investment is reasonably straightforward and easy to understand when compared to business and shares.

We all live in one, have grown up in one and many of us have rented, bought or sold one. You may not know the specifics about exactly what, where and when to buy just yet, but if you stick to a few simple rules of buying close to cities, work, transport, leisure and water, you probably won't go too far wrong.

The more you get to understand property, the more you can purchase and hold on to it. Professionals take it to a different level and find the better properties in suburbs that appreciate quicker than others.

Property is safe

When investing in an asset there's nothing more solid than choosing one that the government and banking system fully support.

Banks love property. They're so sure that bricks and mortar will continue to rise over the long term that they'll lend some young homebuyers 100% of the purchase price – *now that's confidence!* If the banks are happy to lend you the money it is their way of acknowledging the investment is not risky. If it's not risky for them then it shouldn't be risky for you. As the banks are so heavily lent into property they have got to make it work or their whole lending system collapses.

The same goes for the government, because all voters live in houses (ie. they buy or they rent). Therefore the government has got to keep property within reasonable bounds because if every borrower was forced into the street, the national economy would collapse, the government would fall and who knows what the international consequences would be?

Property is the basis of western capitalism, and governments cannot allow it to crash. The US is a case in point with the sub-prime crisis where many people who couldn't afford loans were given them. Certain parts of the American property market collapsed and the government's response was to drop interest rates and keep dropping them until the market reached a stable equilibrium. They will do it for property, but if a blue chip corporation goes to the wall, the government won't move the economy to make sure your shares are okay.

So what does that tell you?

The government is so keen to get our youth into property it gives them First Home Owner Grants to pay all of the expenses involved in purchasing a property and gives them all the stamp duty free of charge too. In some states that adds up to $25k of incentives!

Property is stable

One thing that keeps the residential market stable is that lots of individual people have all got little amounts of property, which creates a patchwork effect of stability. Big conglomerates don't buy entire suburbs and they don't manipulate the market in that way, otherwise suburbs would go to the wall if the conglomeration does. A corporation would rather buy one $100 million building and manage that rather than hundreds of houses peppered around a locality, because 300 houses requires too much finicky work for the big end of town. And that makes property more stable.

Real estate remains strong because:

- *people who live in their house for 10, 20 or 30 years create stability*

- *only 2–3 properties are up for sale in a street at the same time, which means demand is tight*

- *some people won't sell their home at any price, and if there's a limited amount of stock prices rise.*

Because most people don't really know exactly what their property is worth on a day-by-day basis, they don't panic as shareholders in a volatile market might; they simply don't notice short term falls, they just remain where they are. If you've owned the family home for 30 years you wouldn't be aware of what it's worth on a week-by-week basis because you're not selling, and as long as you continue to meet your mortgage payments you won't feel the market fluctuations.

Median House Prices since 1986

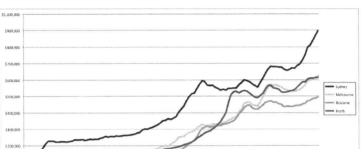

Source data : www.sqmresearch.com.au and Australian Bureau of Statistics

As with all statistics if you ask three different companies for median house prices over the last 20 years they all come out with different numbers. However the trend is clear. They say property tends to double every 7–10 years which indicates an annual growth rate of 7–10%. The statistics from the SQM Research and the Australian Bureau of Statistics over the last 20 years show growth rates between 8–9.3% for the main cities.

Compare the stability of property values compared to the way shares rise and fall on a daily basis as seen on the graph below. The graph shows last week's change. It's at the time of writing and hasn't been specifically picked.

Seeing investment values change constantly can be stressful
(ASX 22.5.08 - time of going to print)

Property is also more solid than paper investments as it's very rarely worth nothing. Remember the dot.com boom when one day shares were valued at $billions then they were valued at nothing overnight? Whereas no matter how bad things get, property always has some worth. Even if the house burns down, the land will still hold its value especially around cities, leisure facilities and water.

Property leverages your money

One of the great advantages that property has over other investments is that you can leverage your money five to ten times fairly safely. High income earners buying their first few properties will often be able to borrow 90–100% of the funds from the bank. Investors tend to borrow 80% when building a large portfolio and those who are nearing retirement might reduce their borrowings to around 40–50% or below.

So for each $200k you have to invest, you can typically buy a $1m property which might grow at a rate of $70–100k per year. You might need to tip some cash in each year to balance the rent and mortgage payments but that's probably only a fraction of what you earned in capital growth (see Chapter 4 for more on this).

In the investment world there is an ongoing debate on the relative merits of property or shares. Property companies say that property grows by more than shares and share companies say that shares rise by more than property.

So I checked out the Australian Stock Exchange website (a company that you would assume is more biased towards promoting shares) and in one of their independent reports they were quoting a 20 year gross average return to 2006 of 11.1% for shares and 11.7% for property. So that would make you think, 'passive investing in property gives me a slightly higher financial return than investing in shares'. But let's do the maths as you will find that you're making twice the money in property because it's normal to be leveraged twice as much. For example:

- *If your $100k buys $200k worth of shares, and that $200k goes up by 13% you'll make $26k.*

- *If your $100k in property buys you $500k worth of property and that goes up by 10% you'll make $50k.*

So even if the share market does slightly outperform property (and I'm not agreeing that it does!), if you've got twice as much leverage in property the share market needs to be going up at 20% consistently to even be near making the same kind of money!

To realise that profit you'll need to sell your shares whereas with property you can often get tax back on your cash flow losses and you can access the capital growth tax free by refinancing. Using the example above:

- *Your $26k profit from shares may reduce to $13k.*

- *Your $50k profit from property can be extracted tax free until you decide to sell.*

Therefore you might actually need four times the return from shares to make the same money as property. If you can earn $50k from property without paying the tax then that's the same as earning $100k and paying 50% tax. If you only invested $100k to buy the $500k property and you make the equivalent of $100k from it then that's a 100% return on your money!

To fairly evaluate the true picture to the nearest dollar you need to add in:

- *the cash flow you need to put into property to balance the mortgage and the rent*

- *the margin calls you might get with shares*

- *the buying, selling and refinancing costs*

- *your ability to get the average return for shares and property*

- *actual tax payable*

- *the volatility of both markets.*

The big picture remains the same, though there's more leverage in property and so you need two to four times the return in shares.

Property is a steady investment

In March, 2008, I was part of a four week stock picking competition in the *Sun Herald* newspaper. Among others, I was up against an astrologer, a chartist, a *Financial Review* financial journalist, a schoolboy and a dart board. We had to pick 10 stocks each and in the first week all our portfolios had dropped by as much as 18%. The remarkable news was that with all that perceived knowledge from the experts the portfolio that won was the one that was picked by the astrologer! This either suggests that shares are governed by the astral constellations or that winning in shares is more hit-and-miss than most people choose to admit.

Property is a steadier investment and the rule of thumb with residential property is that it tends to rise by 7–10% pa over the long term. That means that some properties may rise by 10–15% and others by 0–10% giving an average of 7–10%.

If the reason for that rise comes down to supply and demand then you can reasonably assume that if you invest in property 5–15km from a major city where there is a lot of work (driving wages up) and an attraction to the leisure facilities, then you are more likely to get higher growth than you would in the middle of the Northern Territory where land is not a scarce resource and there isn't a high demand for housing.

The annual summary figures show that the same suburbs that have grown in the past consistently rise in the future. Sure, some people will always buy in the more remote low growth areas for lifestyle or work-related reasons but these are not investment purchases. As an investor if you are making cold hard financial decisions and targeting high growth areas then it shouldn't be too hard for you to beat the national average if you play the long game.

Property doesn't have margin calls

As long as you can meet your mortgage repayments on a property, the banks are unlikely to review your loans even if the market falls. It's very hard for them to really know what your property is worth unless a valuer does a physical inspection and compares it to similar ones that have sold over the last few months. Even when customers have bought property with a 100% loan and the market has dropped the next day putting them into negative equity overnight, the banks are still generally content to ride out the wave as long as the monthly mortgage is met.

As with overdraft facilities, it is written into most mortgage contracts that banks can revalue properties, but they usually don't because if property suddenly dropped 10% and the banks announced to all their borrowers to meet the margin call it would create havoc. The US sub-prime crisis in 2007–2008 has shown that if masses of mortgage customers can't meet their payments and their properties get repossessed it affects the whole economy. So why risk the wider economic repercussions if the mortgage payments are being met? Better for them to hold tight and wait for the market to bounce back, which it has always done in the past.

The US sub-prime market has had a dramatic effect on shares though and this is where margin calls can be frightening. Many shareholders lost 25%+ of their wealth and were forced to liquidate their portfolios in early 2008 as banks required daily margin calls. Being a forced seller of any asset will never get you a good price.

Property leverages your time

Property is one of the most passive investments you can buy which is great if you value the limited time you have away from work. While it does take some time and skill to find and negotiate each property purchase, once bought property takes very little time to manage on an ongoing basis.

I always try to keep my properties in top condition as I have found that preventative maintenance is cheaper and less hassle than having tenants repeatedly complain about ongoing problems. Choosing a good property manager is a key part of owning a portfolio as they can relieve you of all the work.

As a first home buyer in the early days I couldn't afford to pay someone to install a smoke alarm and would do it myself, but now – as a high income earner – I know that my time is better spent elsewhere. I usually instruct my property managers to go ahead and fix a repair if it costs less than $500, and if it costs more than that, to send me an email but get on and fix it anyway.

As soon as I buy, I renovate the property where necessary which means that often there will be no more repairs or maintenance for years to come. It also gives me an instant profit, as spending $80k may increase my property's value by $100k and I can use that equity to help fund any negative cash flow.

Most property owners get emotional about spending money on their properties whereas I see it as looking after my investment. On a $1m property my interest bill is around $70k/year and my repairs/maintenance/strata runs at about $10k/year. Those repairs are an insignificant cost in comparison to the interest and so even if I could do the maintenance work myself my time is better spent with my family or in seeking another property to buy.

Tenants pay most of your mortgage

Tenants are an essential part of owning a property portfolio as they pay your mortgage, yet many property owners see them as a liability. If you buy good properties in good areas you generally attract good tenants. And if you keep your property well maintained and better than your competitors' tenants will stay longer. The majority of rental properties are in a rundown condition and so tenants recognise a good thing when they are onto one.

If you own a premium property it's in a property manager's interest to put in reliable tenants who pay their rent on time as they don't want the hassle or grief of chasing arrears every month. Also if you have a portfolio of properties with the one manager they have too much to lose if they don't look after you properly. They won't want your business going elsewhere.

I always recommend taking out landlord's insurance policies to cover malicious damage and rental gaps due to tenants not keeping to their side of the contract. For the sake of a few hundred dollars it gives you great peace of mind.

Having the right property managed by a good agent and with an insurance policy in place guarantees you always get your rent.

You don't have to sell property to get the cash

One of the main reasons to invest in property is because of its tax efficiency over other investments. With most investments you receive an income plus a capital growth element and typically pay almost 50% tax on any profit.

With an investment strategy that targets high capital growth properties you receive a 4–5% rental income and on average may pay around 7–9% mortgage interest, giving you a loss of about 2–5%. This loss can be offset against your salary income which means you get a tax credit back of around 1–2% which helps fund the negative cash flow.

Rental income	4–5%
Less: mortgage interest	(7–9%)
Equals: loss before tax	(2–5%)
Tax credit	1–3%

The real benefit though is in the capital gain. If your property grows by 10% or $100k most people think that you have to sell that property to realise the cash, but you don't.

If you sell a property to realise the profit, all of that profit disappears in selling costs and capital gains tax. The smarter and more tax efficient way of realising gain is to simply refinance – go to your bank, explain that your property has risen in value and take a loan out against the difference. Your debt will have risen but the amount is virtually the same as if you sold and re-bought elsewhere. Refiancing will be subject to passing the banks serviceability requirements.

By refinancing you are accessing your profits without having to pay tax until you do sell (if you ever do). You're leveraging your money even further by using the bank loan and the money you would have paid in tax to increase your portfolio. Chapter 5 has a detailed example of how the numbers work.

As the tax laws are constantly changing please note that any tax benefits on investments should always be seen as the icing on the cake rather than a reason to invest. The tax efficiencies are a bonus. You should primarily invest in property because it leverages your time and money and it is a safe, solid asset.

Why property?

In summary I believe property investing is a great way to build wealth because it is a safe, solid asset that doesn't bounce up and down in value. It is tax efficient as you get a tax rebate on the cash flow losses and your capital gains are tax free until you sell. In the meantime you can leverage the equity.

And, as with all investments, property does rise and fall as other economic factors change. Property tends to rise for a number of years, fall slightly, flatten for a couple of years and then it rises again. So the key with property is to have enough cash flow to support it in the short term, as it's almost guaranteed to rise in the long term.

REALITY CHECK

Do you feel that in the long term,
residential property is a good investment?

◯ Yes   ◯ No

Do you know people who own two or more
properties?

◯ Yes   ◯ No

Do you feel comfortable with the idea of
owning a property that somebody else is
living in?

◯ Yes   ◯ No

Are you at all concerned by the fluctuating
nature of the share market?

◯ Yes   ◯ No

If you've answered 'yes' to any of these questions, keep reading.

4

The portfolio approach to property investment

When most people purchase property they are buying their family home which is nearly always an emotional decision. As their income goes up they upgrade the family house for a more expensive one in a better suburb. And if they have excess income, they might also purchase a holiday home or a weekender, which again tends to be an equally emotional decision.

Most people make great choices when they're buying their family home because they're going to live in it and they understand the street, the suburb and the town. Having made such a great decision fills them with too much confidence. However, when it comes to making an investment purchase, instead of getting independent professional advice, they fly to an unfamiliar town and buy property on intuition. After all, the family home was a smart purchase, why not this one too?

If you decide to invest in property as a wealth creation strategy, the first thing to learn is that property is now your 'business' and all decisions should be financial and unemotional. In this chapter I want to share some of the different property investing options available to you and their pros and cons, so that you can develop a wealth creation strategy that's right for you.

You're dealing with large amounts of money, so you need to understand what to buy and what not to buy. You can't just buy any property and expect a spectacular result because even if property doubles on average every 7–10 years, some properties might creep up by just 5% whereas others could rise an impressive 15%.

Direct versus indirect property

Owning a residential property in your own name (direct property) which you control 100% is generally the safest way to buy property because:

- *You can value it today.*

- *You can get a tenant today.*

- *You can get a mortgage today.*

- *You control it by yourself.*

And so only a limited amount of things can go wrong. As soon as you start investing with other people the risks start increasing. Buying your family home is a form of investing in direct property but every time you upgrade to another location you throw away tens or hundreds of thousands of dollars in buying and selling costs. The idea of investing in direct property is to buy the right property that is worth hanging onto for years. The great thing about direct property is you get to choose what property you buy. Even if the property temporarily falls in value, as long as you keep up the mortgage repayments the bank shouldn't force you to sell it.

Property trusts

The main form of investing in indirect property is listed property trusts or Real Estate Investment Trust (REIT), which is similar to investing in shares except the underlying asset is commercial/industrial/retail property rather than a company.

Because you're buying a share in a trust the entry costs are a lot smaller than buying a whole property yourself but because you don't own the whole thing, it's not under your control. And so, just like the share market, your investment may be subject to the same volatility and the same chance of going bust.

When buying into a property trust you have to trust that the fund manager is making good decisions and fully acting in your interests. If the share value of the trust falls it may well lead to a margin call if you have borrowed against it. You also can't leverage as much into property trusts as you can into direct property and that means you're not likely to make as much money.

Residential versus commercial/industrial/retail

The reason I prefer residential property rather than commercial, industrial and retail is that non-residential properties fluctuate with the economy so you've got to be quite skilled to predict future trends. One example is the recent retail shift in Sydney where the trendiest strip used to be Oxford Street, Paddington, then it moved to King Street, Newtown. There have been similar shifts in Perth, Brisbane, Melbourne and Adelaide.

Residential property is not subject to such market whims as once a residential area is built up it hardly changes. Residential houses are not sold to build commercial places, it's invariably the other way round. So residential is the most stable, solid market because once there's infrastructure like schools and transport, people stay.

I like residential because the capital growth is generally pretty consistent, so is the rent. The rent may vary from 4% to 5% but it usually remains in that range whereas commercial, retail or industrial could fluctuate wildly, just like the share market. As the value of commercial/industrial/retail property is based on the rent it receives, often the way to make money is to buy something that is unlet and then find a blue chip tenant to occupy it. It's a speculative market that takes more skill and knowledge to be successful.

Positive cash flow versus capital gain

There's an ongoing debate in property circles as to whether you are better off investing in positive cash flow property (which gives you a high rental yield) or negatively geared or negative cash flow properties (which typically give you a high capital gain).

If you're a high income earner, I believe that the quickest way to build wealth is through capital gain because it is tax free until you sell and that gain can be leveraged to fund more properties.

Positive cash flow properties are typically found in rural areas, they are slightly cheaper and might have 10% rental yield and only 5% capital gain. The argument for them is that they constantly put money in your pocket and there's no limit to how many you can hold, as they don't drain your cash flow. The reality is that they may not grow much in value and so may take ages to fund your next deposit. You are primarily investing in them for rental income and as that income is taxed, you'll need a lot of properties to give you any kind of wealth or passive income.

Negatively geared properties are generally closer to major cities and might typically have a 5% rental yield and 10% capital gain. The argument against them is that there is a limit on how many you can hold as they drain your cash flow. This isn't typically a problem for high income earners as they do have spare cash and you can always use the capital gain to fund the cash flow by simply refinancing. These properties are great for creating wealth because by definition their prime aim is to grow in value.

So let's work out the numbers to see what's best if you have $1m to invest.

Positive cash flow

Rental income $1m x 10%	$100,000
Mortgage interest $1m x 8%	($80,000)
Profit before tax	$20,000
Profit after tax	$10,000
Capital gain $1m x 5%	$50,000
Total return $10,000 + $50,000	**$60,000**

Negative geared

Rental income $1m x 5%	$50,000
Mortgage interest $1m x 8%	($80,000)
Profit/(loss) before tax	($30,000)
Profit/(loss) after tax	($15,000)
Capital gain $1m x 10%	$100,000
Total return ($15,000) + $100,000	**$85,000**

The capital gain property will create more wealth because the majority of the profit is untaxed. It would be taxed on sale of the property which may never eventuate and the equity can be leveraged in the meantime. The main reason that the majority of the population choose to invest in positive cash flow properties is the fact that they cannot cash flow the $15,000 difference between the rent and the mortgage. As long as you can cash flow this in the short term, you should make more money in the long term. That is why it's an investment strategy exclusively for high income earners.

House versus unit

The saying 'land appreciates and buildings depreciate' gives people the impression they should always buy houses over units because houses have a greater land component. Land is a scarce resource and therefore rises in value according to a corresponding rise in demand.

The value of a $1m house might be split between $400k for the land and $600k for the value of the building. Whereas in a $1m unit the land size is obviously smaller and so wouldn't rise as much.

Logic then suggests to always buy a house.

However, if you go to some suburbs, like Bondi Beach in Sydney or St Kilda in Melbourne, buying a house might cost around $3 million. While that's good because there's a lot of land which will appreciate, not many people can afford to rent it at 5% because that would equate to $3,000 a week.

Most people who can afford to pay $3,000 a week rent can normally afford to buy their own home and they do so because they can then enjoy all the advantages of home ownership including being able to decorate it as they wish. So rather than getting 5% rent or $3,000 per week, that property might only get 2.5% rent or $1,500 because only a limited amount of people could rent it at that price.

If you can get 12% capital growth on a house rather than 10% on a unit you will make more profit from the house but if you only get 2.5% rent then the difference between the rent and the mortgage might be too much to cash flow.

Let's compare buying a $3m house with 3 x $1m units.

	$3m house	**3 x $1m units**
Rental income 2.5/5%	$75k	$150k
Mortgage interest at 8%	($240k)	($240k)
Profit/(loss) before tax	($165k)	($90k)
Profit/(loss) after tax	**($83k)**	**($45k)**
Capital growth 12/10%	$360k	$300k
Total return	**$277k**	**$255k**

Similar to the prior positive cash flow versus capital calculation, the property with the higher capital gain will generate more wealth. A house should give you more capital growth than owning a unit in the same suburb but this is all dependent on being able to cash flow the bigger loss.

If the property market was going through a flat period and you had to fund $83k of losses for a number of years the financial or emotional strain might be too much to shoulder compared to losing $45k.

I tend to buy houses or units depending on the median price of property where I am investing. I would typically buy a unit if I was investing in Sydney or Melbourne but a house if I was investing in Brisbane or Perth as that's where 80% of the population tends to live in those cities.

Home state versus interstate

Should you buy in your suburb or invest elsewhere?

> 🔹 *The advantage of buying locally is you're less likely to get ripped off because you understand the market and you roughly know the property values.*

> 🔹 *The disadvantage is that unless you live in a high capital growth area your property value won't significantly increase.*

If you don't live in a high capital growth suburb you should consider buying elsewhere. The disadvantage with that is you are unlikely to understand interstate property values, so you're definitely going to need property valuers and building inspectors to double-check what you're proposing to buy and how much you intend to pay.

Normally you need to see 50–100 properties to understand local value and to recognise what is a good property and what isn't. If you live in Sydney and want to buy in Brisbane, you can't fly up and expect to understand the whole local market in a couple of days (ie what side of the street is good, what side of the street is bad, etc) and buy a property in one weekend. This is where you will need to use a buyer's agent with specialist knowledge of the locality.

Furthermore, if you want to buy six properties in six different areas, there's no way you're going to see 500–600 properties. You've got to delegate to the professionals. Spending $20k–$30k on buyer's agents' fees is a good investment because their fee is only 2%–3% of the property value which they will save by buying you a better property at a cheaper price.

New versus second hand

One reason to buy new property is that you get a huge depreciation allowance as the wear and tear on the building, fixtures and fittings can be offset against tax. The Tax Office lets you apportion the wear and tear over a period of 40 years for buildings and maybe 5–15 years for the fixtures and fittings. Second hand properties are usually fully depreciated and so you won't get that benefit.

Often the sellers of new properties use various methods to rip off unsuspecting buyers. You should never buy an investment purely for tax reasons as you need to consider the big picture. Many developers mark up new property prices and then market them as 'own a property for less than $50 per week' as the tax credits you get back on the paper depreciation losses reduce the difference between the rent and the mortgage. If the property has been over priced by 10%, it's not worth paying an extra $100k just to get a few thousand back in tax.

These properties may come with rental guarantees for a few years which inexperienced investors think makes them risk free. Often the rent has been artificially inflated so again you overpay for the property. Adding an extra $100 per week to a guaranteed rent would cost them $5,000 per year for a few years but might net them an extra $100k on the sale price.

Often the company making the rental guarantee is a $2 company and not capable of guaranteeing the rent. When the property owner runs into trouble because they don't have a tenant, the guarantor has empty pockets, and the property owners (who were relying on this guarantee) have to stand on their own. If you follow this route, make sure you know who is providing the guarantee!

They might even justify the inflated prices with examples of other properties they've sold at higher prices. But just because they've conned other buyers into paying their price doesn't mean the property is worth it. I always compare it to similar properties in other blocks and especially to what I can buy second hand as the vendors are less likely to be able to play with those figures.

A downside of buying a new property is that everyone falls in love with it because it's perfect – people think they could buy it tomorrow and rent it out straight away. It might be hassle free but for that you're probably going to pay a high price.

Inspecting a second hand property that has been lived in for the last 30 years with the same carpet, curtains and everything else unchanged (and it stinks), most inexperienced buyers will not be able to see through the smells and the bad carpet to see how it could be transformed. Also they haven't got the time, energy and know-how to put into it. They wouldn't know whether to spend $20k, $50k or $100k on renovations. Buying second hand creates an opportunity for those who have the knowledge and ability, or are willing to delegate the buying process to someone who has.

An advantage of buying new properties is that you can buy them off the plan. As long as you buy at the right price you might be able to secure a $1m property that will be worth $1.2m when built two years later. Rather than having to put all the money down now you often need to just put down 5–10% and that can even be a deposit bond or bank guarantee. These are like insurance policies which guarantee you will pay the deposit on completion. As long as you have equity in another property you can often get a $50k bond for about $2,000–$3,000. Earning $200k from a $2,000 deposit is a great return on investment. However, like all properties, off the plan sales can fall as well as rise, so caution needs to be taken.

An advantage of second hand properties over new ones is that you can add value to them by renovating. A simple paint and recarpeting job can cost as little as $5,000 while adding as much as $10k–$20k to a property's value, and doing a complete refurbishment for $80k may add $100k to its value. The key is to make sure you know what adds value without overcapitalising and ensuring you have the right team of professionals to do the job. This can be tricky if you're inexperienced or are just doing a single project, so consider delegating to a professional project manager.

Holiday homes

Many high income earners purchase holiday homes as investments thinking that they'll get the benefit of the property when it's not in use. I tend to think of holiday homes as luxuries rather than investments.

Owners typically want to use such a place in peak times which is precisely when everyone else wants it too. This clashes with the best times to get rental income to pay for the rest of the year's mortgage. Rental incomes can be quite volatile and unless you are strict with your budgeting you may find yourself paying a second mortgage with virtually no income coming in.

Holiday homes are often located in towns which are heavily reliant on tourism for income. This could mean the town is more vulnerable to economic downturns and changes in laws. The same risk applies to properties in mining towns or those occupied by the Armed Services.

I prefer to invest my money in the safest place for property, which is around major cities with a range of industries as with this comes consistent rent and solid capital growth. Having my money work harder for me allows me to rent wherever I choose, going on holiday whenever I feel and often in a place much better than I could afford to buy.

Diversification

Just like it makes good investment sense to diversify your wealth creation strategy across a balance of property shares and cash, it also makes good sense to diversify your investment within the overall property market.

Owning one single high value property may make it easier to manage but if something goes wrong or if you find it hard to tenant, all of your financial eggs are in one large basket. Diversifying your property portfolio across a number of smaller value properties in different geographical areas should ensure that most are fully tenanted and that you don't face any unforeseen issues. It should also ensure that where some properties are falling in value, others are rising.

A portfolio of several properties takes more to manage than a single one but for a small percentage of the rent you can outsource the management to a professional property manager. S/he will deal with all of the tenant and maintenance issues and also prepare a financial summary for your accountant. To me, that's money well spent.

The perfect property portfolio

Different people prefer different property investment strategies depending on their knowledge, attitude to risk and how much they want to be involved.

If you are a high income earner who wants to create passive wealth quickly while reducing your risk as much as possible then I believe the best strategy is to buy properties that:

1. are 5k–15k from major cities as they are close to transport, leisure and work and the scarcity of land underpins the value. CBDs have no height restrictions so technically there is no limit to supply, whereas suburbs usually have height restrictions

2. are within 10%–20% of the median price for that area as that means 80% of the population can afford to rent them, ie $900k–$1.2m range

3. suit the median price for that area, ie, a house in Queensland, South Australia, Western Australia or unit in New South Wales or Victoria

4. are a mix of new off-the-plan properties to get growth with little deposit and second hand properties that can be renovated to add immediate value

5. have two bedrooms, as they are more attractive to well paid professionals who may rent them. Not many professionals will share with three under the same roof. Also it's easier to get two people each paying $500 per week than it is to get one person paying $700–$800 per week for a one bedroom unit or studio. Houses could have four bedrooms and any property I buy definitely needs to have parking

6. are in smaller blocks as they are unique since there's usually less up for rent at any one time. Big blocks have big strata levies with expensive lifts, pools and gyms which don't give you any more rent or capital growth. As soon as someone else more desperate than you knocks down the rent or reduces their sale price for a quick sale, every other property in the block gets devalued

7. have plenty of sunlight, are on quiet streets and are walking distance to either shops, leisure facilities or water. I avoid being too close to industrial/commercial/ retail premises such as schools, churches, factories, etc

8. are likely to grow steadily for evermore. While it's great to buy at a discount, it's the return I get year after year that really matters

9. in proven areas of capital growth, or areas you know well. It may be more exotic to buy interstate or to take a punt on an up-and-coming suburb but by investing in proven areas you're putting less at risk and guaranteeing a more solid return. Plus your knowledge of that area is what will give you a competitive edge over other buyers, ensuring you don't buy in the worst street in the suburb, or on the wrong side of the road

10. bought for capital growth.

REALITY CHECK

Do you believe in seeking professional
advice for any major financial decision?

☐ Yes   ☐ No

Do you accept that some investment
advice can be largely in the interests of the
investment adviser?

☐ Yes   ☐ No

Do you believe that 'gut feel' has only
a limited part to play in investment
decisions?

☐ Yes   ☐ No

If it meant you were able to finance an
investment property, could you 'find'
$1,000–$2,000 a month – either from your
salary or from the equity in your property?

☐ Yes   ☐ No

Do you prefer to spread risk over a number
assets rather than concentrate it in just
one?

☐ Yes   ☐ No

If you've answered 'yes' to any of these questions, keep reading.

5

The numbers and why most people get them wrong

5

Having a personal property portfolio combines the advantages of buying property with having a share portfolio. It's a bit of a mixture of the two in that you build up a diversified portfolio through acquiring lots of smaller assets to get income and capital growth from multiple sources. Even if there is short term volatility in the market and one property doesn't grow or has a temporary issue (like not receiving the rent) it will combine with the rest of the assets and your wealth still grows.

Calculating the profit breakeven point

When you buy property you will have to pay stamp duty and legal fees which typically equate to 5% of the purchase costs, so a $1m property will actually cost you $1,050k in total. Whether you borrow money to buy the property or pay cash, there will always be an opportunity cost of any money you put down as a deposit and so for the purposes of the following calculations we will assume that all monies are borrowed.

To make things simple tax is assumed at 50%. The other numbers we have used are generalisations at the time of writing and so I suggest you take these numbers to your accountant and get them checked for your specific circumstances. Your accountant can then give you different scenarios based on interest rates and rising and falling rents so you can have a complete picture of what may happen in the future. If you can make a profit from the worst case scenario, things can only get better!

- *If you buy a $1m 2-bedroom unit in a popular suburb you should be aiming to get about $900–$1,000 per week rent. This equates to about 4.5%–5% return (900 x 50 weeks divided by $1m). So at 4.5% return, each year you would get $45k in rental income.*

- *If a $1m unit plus stamp duty and legals costs you $1,050k and you borrow all of the money at 9% interest it will cost you $95k in mortgage payments.*

- *To pay for the annual maintenance, strata fees, water and property management it is likely to cost you on average 1% of the property's value = $10k per year.*

To work out a couple of scenarios I have used $900 per week rent with 9% interest and $1,000 per week rent with 8% interest. Your annual profit and loss statement for the property will look something like this:

Good   Better

	Good	Better
Rental income ($900/1,000 x 50)	$45k	$50k
Mortgage interest ($1,050k x 9%/8%)	($95k)	($84k)
Other expenses ($1m x 1%)	($10k)	($10k)
Loss before tax	($60k)	($44k)

If interest rates are less than 8-9%, you make more (but I always like to err on the side of caution).

If you are a high income earner you should be able to offset that loss against your normal income and therefore get a tax credit back which would reduce your loss to:

Loss after tax ($60k/$44k x 50%)	($30k)	($22k)

If covering the loss from your income is a challenge then read on as there are options available to be able to sustain your portfolio growth.

If a property makes a loss, why buy it?

In Chapter 3 we discussed the pros and cons of positive cash flow versus capital gain properties and we concluded that paying for a cash flow negative property would more than likely give us a higher capital gain which is better for long term wealth creation.

If the property rises by 10% we make:

	Good	Better
Total return (($30k)/($22k) + $100k)	$70k	$78k

But what does the property have to rise by (ie what is its breakeven point), to make a profit?

That's calculated by:

Loss after tax	$30k/$22k		
——————— =	——————— =	3.0%	2.2%
Property value	$1m		

So the question you need to ask is, *Do I think property will rise by more than 2.2% –3.0% in the long term?*

If the answer is 'yes' then buying should be a good decision.

If the answer is 'no' then you shouldn't buy as you won't make a profit.

Err on the side of caution

I always prefer to look at the worst case scenario and so with these figures, I assume that I may not receive a tax credit back on any losses, ie, what if the government removes negative gearing? So I also suggest working out your breakeven point before tax.

Loss before tax	$60k/$44k		
——————— =	——————— =	6.0%	4.4%
Property value	$1m		

These figures are certainly higher.

My personal opinion is that this really is a worst case scenario and if you read on further, you will learn the true reality of the decision in hand.

Cash flowing the loss

If you are happy with the breakeven points above, the main necessity is to be able to cash flow the losses in the short term as capital gains may only be seen in the long term. While many high income earners may be able to cash flow these losses from their excess salaries others may prefer to have their property portfolios as stand-alone investments that take care of themselves.

You should think of property as a business where one division makes a profit (capital growth of property) and the other makes a loss (your rent minus your mortgage). A business owner doesn't fund the loss-making division from their wages, they simply offset one division's profit against the other division's loss and then pocket the difference. Property can be seen in the same light. Rather than fund the loss from your wages, why not fund it from the capital gain?

With a similar thought process, do all new businesses make a profit in the first few years of operation? No, many new businesses take a few years to make a profit and so an investor injects working capital into the business as part of the initial investment. Property is similar, it makes a loss at the start and so on top of the purchase price you usually need to invest some working capital.

So rather than a $1m property costing $1,050k with buying costs, perhaps you should think of it as costing $1.2m which would give you $150k in working capital.

Then the figures would look like this:

	Good	**Better**
Rental income ($900/$1,00 x 50)	$44k	$50k
Mortgage interest ($1.2m x 9%/8%)	($108k)	($96k)
Other expenses ($1m x 1%)	($10k)	($10k)
Loss before tax	($74k) 7.4% b/e	($56k) 5.6% b/e
Loss after tax ($74k/$56k x 50%)	($37k) 3.7% b/e	($28k) 2.8% b/e

If you've borrowed an extra $150k of working capital and your negative cash flow was $28–$37k per year, you could last 4–5 years without having to use any of your own money. So at the end of 4–5 years your total borrowings will be $1.2m and your property should be worth:

Growth	Yr0	Yr1	Yr2	Yr3	Yr4	Yr5
7%	$1,000k	$1,070k	$1,145k	$1,225k	$1,311k	$1,403k
10%	$1,000k	$1,100k	$1,210k	$1,331k	$1,464k	$1,611k

In 4–5 years your wealth will have increased between:

- *$110k ($1,310k less $1,200k borrowings – 7% growth over 4 years)*

- *$411k ($1,611k less $1,200k borrowings – 10% growth over 5 years).*

If you left the $150k in an offset account you would only pay interest on the money as you withdrew it, so your interest on day one would actually be calculated on $1,050k and not $1,200k which means that your costs would be less and the above example is again a worst case scenario.

At the end of 4–5 years, if the property has risen by $311k–$611k you could go back to your lender and refinance part of that equity out and use the cash for future working capital and/or to use as a deposit on another property.

Building a whole portfolio

Banks are not going to lend you $1.2m on a $1m property so how do property investors do it?

As a general rule most banks will lend up to 80% of a median priced residential property which on a $1m property equals $800k. You then need to come up with $400k:

- *$200k deposit (20% of $1m)*

- *$50k costs (5% of $1m)*

- *$150k buffer/working capital (or whatever you think is appropriate).*

Most investors use the equity that they have built up in their own home or another investment property to finance that $400k. If you had a property worth $2m that was paid off and you wanted to push your investments to your limit you could:

- *borrow 80% = $1.6m*

- *split that $1.6m into four lots of $400k*

- *purchase 4 x $1m properties = $4m.*

Your total assets/debt position would be:

- *$1.6m mortgage on your main residence*

- *4 x $800k = $3.2m debt on your 4 investment properties*

- *total debt = $4.8m*

- *total assets = $2m + 4 x $1m = $6m (80% geared)*

- *buffer 4 x $150k = $600k.*

Your new figures would look like this:

	Good	Better
Rental income ($900/$1,000 x 50 x 4)	$180k	$200k
Mortgage interest ($1.2m x 9%/8% x 4)	($432k)	($384k)
Other expenses ($1m x 1% x 4)	($40k)	($40k)
Loss before tax	($292k) 7.3%	($224k) 5.6%
Loss after tax ($292k/$112k x 50%)	($146k) 3.7%	($112k) 2.8%

If you've borrowed an extra $600k of working capital and your negative cash flow was $112k–146k per year, you could last 4–5 years without having to use any of your own money. So at the end of 4–5 years your total borrowings will be $4.8m and your property should be worth:

Growth	Yr0	Yr1	Yr2	Yr3	Yr4	Yr 5
7%	$4m	$4.3m	$4.6m	$4.9m	$5.2m	$5.6m
10%	$4m	$4.4m	$4.8m	$5.3m	$5.9m	$6.4m

While these are larger amounts, in percentage terms nothing has really changed as you have just bought four lots of the same investment we calculated before. Using the equity in your own home and none of your own money or wages, in 4–5 years your wealth will have increased between:

- *$400k ($5.2m less $4.8m borrowings – 7% growth)*

- *$1.6m ($6.4m less $4.8m borrowings – 10% growth).*

The returns may actually be slightly higher if you take into consideration depreciation on your property which is an extra tax deduction (tax credit) and the fact that your buffer would be sitting in an offset account and not costing you interest until you use it.

Funding the negative cash flow from your salary

If you can fund the negative cash flow from excess wages that you are not spending, the returns get even better as you haven't got any money tied up in a buffer.

If you had a property worth $2m that was paid off and you really wanted to push your investments to your limit you could:

- *borrow 80% = $1.6m (use $1.5m and keep $100k buffer)*

- *split that $1.5m into six lots of $250k ($200k deposit + $50k costs)*

- *purchase 6 x $1m properties = $6m.*

Your total assets/debt position would be:

- *$1.5m mortgage on your main residence (6 x $250k)*

- *6 x $800k = $4.8m debt on your six investment properties*

- *total debt = $6.3m*

- *total assets = $2m + 6 x $1m = $8m (79% geared)*

- *buffer = $100k.*

Your new figures would look like this:

	Good	**Better**
Rental income ($900/$1,000 x 50 x 6)	$270k	$300k
Mortgage interest ($1,050k x 9%/8% x 6)	($567k)	($504k)
Other expenses ($1m x 1% x 6)	($60k)	($60k)
Loss before tax	($357k) 5.95%	($264k) 4.4%
Loss after tax ($357k/$264k x (50%)	($179k) 3.0%	($132k) 2.2%

At the end of 4–5 years your total borrowings will be $6.3m and your property should be worth:

Growth	Yr0	Yr1	Yr2	Yr3	Yr4	Yr 5
7%	$6m	$6.4m	$6.9m	$7.4m	$7.9m	$8.4m
10%	$6m	$6.6m	$7.3m	$8m	$8.8m	$9.7m

In 4–5 years your wealth will have increased between:

- *$1.6m ($7.9m less $6.3m borrowings = 7% growth)*

- *$3.4m ($9.7m less $6.3m borrowings = 10% growth).*

That's a much better result both in terms of increased wealth and also the fact that the breakeven point has reduced to between 2.2% and 3.0%.

Making even more wealth

Rather than refinance at the end of 4–5 years (and use the equity to fund more deposits) there is no reason why you couldn't revalue your portfolio every year to access the available equity. If it's been a flat or downward market you would have to stand still and if there's been a growth phase you could carry on.

How to further reduce the risk

Just because it is possible to leverage to 80% doesn't mean you have to. If you are more risk averse you could use the $800k equity to buy:

- *4 properties with a $150k buffer on each*
  (($1.6m – 1m) / 4)

- *3 properties with a $280k buffer on each*
  (($1.6m – 750k) / 3)

- *2 properties with a $550k buffer on each*
  (($1.6m – 500k) / 2)

- *1 property with a $1.35m buffer ($800k – 250k).*

If your $1m property loses $30–40k per year a $1.35m buffer would last you 30 to 45 years. Now that's a buffer zone!

If you were buying a number of properties it would be prudent to purchase them over an extended time period rather than all at the same time. The same idea is used when buying a large amount of shares. Low cost averaging means that you get an average buying price and so even if the market has fallen you've bought some at the top, some at the middle and some at the bottom.

Don't fear the gear

Being in debt does make you susceptible to rising interest rates and therefore greater overheads. However it's a way of extending your reach. A classic truism with property or investing in general is 'don't fear the gear'. If you want to get wealthy, getting over your fear of debt is probably your biggest hurdle.

The older generation always wanted to pay off their debts because paying interest was seen as bad debt, and they didn't feel totally financially secure until they'd paid off their home loan.

Concentrate on the big picture

Under a normal principal and interest loan it takes most homeowners 25–30 years to pay off their mortgage, which is a long time. If property values tend to double every 7–10 years why not double your debt and buy two properties rather than one?

- *If you change both mortgages to interest-only your repayments will reduce and that will help pay any difference between the rent and mortgage interest on the second property.*

- *If you lease out the second property you will have rental income to help pay the extra mortgage.*

- *In 7–10 years time both properties should double in value but the mortgages will stay the same because you will have paid the interest.*

- *You could then sell off the second property and use the profit to pay off your first mortgage leaving you debt free in 7–10 years.*

There would be capital gains tax to pay on the profit of the investment property so you may need an extra year or two of growth to cover it. Nevertheless, you're still paying off your mortgage in a fraction of the time.

While being in debt can be seen as increasing your risk, this example shows that while it may be *more* risky in the first few years, once your equity has risen it can actually be *less* risky as your equity is rising and your debt is staying the same.

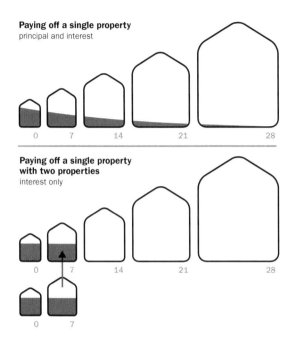

Paying off a single property
principal and interest

0   7   14   21   28

**Paying off a single property
with two properties**
interest only

0   7   14   21   28

0   7

If buying two properties to pay off the first one is a good strategy – then why stop at one? Why not repeat the process? Why not buy 3, 4, 5 or 6 properties? There's nothing wrong with borrowing if you're using the money to buy an appreciating asset. So typically if you bought a $1m property, the downside is yes, it's going to cost you $20k–$40k pa but if the asset is going to grow by $100k a year, you can treat the negative cash flow as the investment into your savings plan!

You've got to look at the big picture and rather than worry about paying more interest, if you're making money – who cares? Each property I buy is going to cost me $2,000–$4,000 per month but at the end of an average year, I should be creaming $80k–$120k.

Fear of debt is the biggest thing to get over. If you're worrying about debt, walk through the numbers with an accountant who specialises in property investing. As long as property continues to grow by at least 3–4% pa – if you can hold on, you will make money. So if you want to make a lot of money you shouldn't be worried about debt because banks, governments and every corporation use debt to grow their business.

Reverse mortgages

Another way to get over your fear of debt is to understand the concept of
reverse mortgages. Reverse mortgages are normally only available to
retirees and are a loan they never have to repay as it comes out of their
estate on death, which is great if they have little or no income and need
more money to live, ie, they are asset rich and cash poor.

If the retiree has a property worth say $1m, the banks know that the property
will typically grow by $50–100k per year. So if they lend them say $25k per
year to live on, even with interest capitalising, the property will always grow
by more than the debt. That enables the retiree to live off the equity created
during their lives and still pass something on to their kids and grandkids.

Cash flow in the long term

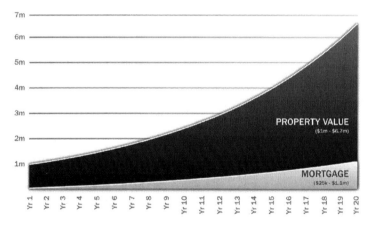

This graph clearly shows that while your debt is increasing by $25k pa plus
interest, your property value is increasing at a greater rate.

Even if you work out the most conservative average property growth you can calculate, what is an appropriate amount of capital to safely withdraw?

If the banks consider living off the equity good enough for you after retirement, why not use the same principle during your lifetime when you still have an income to have a better life and to constantly increase your assets so you have even more for retirement?

Principal and interest versus interest only

The same principles above should be similarly used when considering having an interest-only loan over a principal and interest loan. Most investors use interest-only loans as it improves their cash flow because the repayments are smaller. That enables them to afford to buy more property which makes them more money.

Home owners typically want to pay off the principal and interest repayments so they clear their debt. But the value of the property doesn't rise any quicker whether or not it is debt free and so you're surely better off using the principal part of the repayment to help fund a second property.

Principle and interest payments

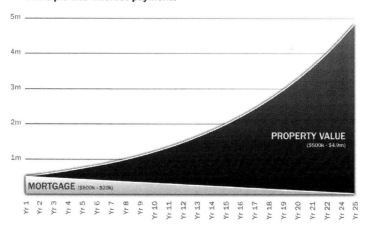

The above graph shows what happens when you borrow $500k to buy a $500k property and you pay it off over 25 years at a consistent rate. At 10% growth your wealth would be around $5m.

Interest only payments

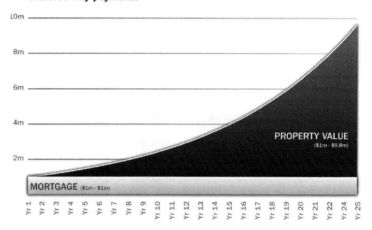

The graph above shows what happens when you buy two properties and only pay an interest-only mortgage. While your debt remains constant at $1m, your two properties rise to $10m, leaving you a net wealth of $9m.

While having more debt is riskier to start with, as soon as the properties grow you can release equity to give you more of a buffer zone to guard against interest rate rises and other expenses.

Never sell

Selling property incurs lots of costs and taxes and often you're going to use the money to buy another property anyway. If you buy the right investment in the first place, why would you ever sell?

If you bought a property for $500k which subsequently rose to $1m, what would happen if you sold it to buy another one? So that we can compare it with the refinancing alternative, let's assume the maximum you could borrow was 80% of the property's value.

- *You buy a $500k property with $100k deposit and $400k mortgage.*

- *It then rises to $1m and you sell it.*

- *Real estate agents fees would be about 2% = $20k.*

- *Capital gains tax would be $1m – $20k fees – $500k cost = $480k x 25% tax = $120k.*

- *Which would leave you with $1m – $20k costs – $120k tax – $400k mortgage = $460k as a deposit and costs on a next property.*

- *If you then bought property worth $1.84m and the bank lent you 80% = $1.47m your deposit would be 20% = $368k.*

- *There would be buying costs of 5% = $92k.*

- *20% deposit = $368k + costs $92k = $460k that you have from the previous property.*

- *Your portfolio is worth $1.84m and potentially rises by $184k per year.*

Property value	$1m
Less: selling fees	($20k)
Less: capital gains tax	($120k)
Less: current mortgage	($400k)
Cash for next deposit	$460k
New properties	$1.84m
Costs	$92k
Less: new mortgage	($1.47m)
Deposit needed	$460k

Annual capital growth $1.84m x 10% = $184k/yr

Rather than selling your property you could simply refinance and use the equity to buy more property without having to pay the selling costs and capital gains tax.

- *If your property is worth $1m and you refinance at 80% the bank would lend $800k.*

- *You already owe $400k so that gives you $400k for deposits and costs for further properties.*

- *If you then bought property worth $1.6m and the bank lends you 80% = $1.28m your deposit would be 20% = $320k.*

- *There would be buying costs of 5% = $80k.*

- *20% deposit = $320k + costs $80k = $400k that you have from the previous property.*

- *Your portfolio is worth $1m + $1.6m = $2.6m and potentially rises by $260k per year.*

Property value	$1m
80% mortgage	$800k
Less: current mortgage	($400k)
Cash for next deposit	$400k
New properties	$1.6m
Costs	$80k
Less: new mortgage	($1.28m)
Deposit needed	$400k

Annual capital growth $2.6m x 10% = $260k/yr

Refinancing rather than selling saves $140k in selling costs and capital gains tax which allows you to buy an extra $760k of property. You would have a tax liability when you do eventually sell but wouldn't you rather earn an extra $76k per year and hold off paying tax for 30 years? You're using the tax money to make even more money.

Buffer zone

So I'm *not* advocating buying and selling property – because the cost of getting in and out is too expensive. The majority of people who have sold a property in the past end up regretting it once they realise what it might be currently worth. They get excited about immediate profits, but they fail to stop and consider the possible growth in the long term.

All we want to do is keep buying property, and as that property rises in value we want a facility to access the growth of our equity as a buffer zone if something should go wrong. So rather than paying the difference between the rent and the mortgage from our wages we want a buffer zone to cover the difference. We want to pay that differential from the profits, so that all the property is self-sustaining.

If you are scared of debt you can choose your level of borrowings and you don't have to borrow as high as 70%–80%. If you're risk averse with a million dollar property you might be comfortable saying, 'I only want to borrow $100k and that's it'. Or you could say, 'I've got a high income, I'm young, I've got a back-up plan, so I'm happy borrowing at 80% because then I can buy lots more property'. The whole idea of building a property portfolio is you don't have to take on large amounts of debt if you don't want to. If you want to purely invest cash, you can just invest the cash.

Many who are reading this have the ability to buy 5–10 properties right now, but they will probably do it gradually and they will cautiously start off with just one. When they're comfortable with the money coming in and out, maybe next year they'll buy a second. You can take on as much, or as little, as you want. If you're dealing with property you can always sell it, and if you bought at the right price ideally you'll make a tidy profit whenever you decide to sell.

Why not rent yourself?

Most high income earners think that renting is for poor people and they would never do it themselves. Rather than accept this generalisation why not check out the numbers and see what the reality is?

If you could borrow $3m and had the choice between buying your own home for $3m or buying three $1m investments and then renting your own home, what would you do?

If you bought your own home that would be simple. It would cost you $3m x 8% mortgage = $240k per year.

If you bought 3 x $1m properties then you should get about 4% rent return ($800 per week each) after expenses. As it's an investment you would get a tax rebate on any losses.

If you then decided to rent a $3m property you would probably only pay about 2% rent as there isn't as much demand for properties that are out of the price range of most people. Therefore it might only cost $60k to rent.

Rent $1m x 3 x 4%	120,000
Mortgage $1m x 3 x 8%	(240,000)
Loss before tax	(120,000)
Loss after tax	(60,000)
Rent on $3m at 2%	(60,000)
Total cost to you	**(120,000)**

By choosing to rent a $3m property it costs you $120k rather than $240k to buy.

Both ways you get to own $3m of property but as the rent returns are often half as much on luxury properties it costs you less. By having investment properties you get the benefit of a tax deduction now rather than later with your own home, which would be capital gains tax free on sale (which may never happen).

Would you rather own a $3m property or rent one worth $9m?

You could actually stretch the boundaries further and buy 3 x $1m properties and rent a $9m property for the same cost as buying a $3m home!

Rent $1m x 3 x 4%	120,000
Mortgage $1m x 3 x 4%	(240,000)
Loss before tax	(120,000)
Loss after tax	(60,000)
Rent on $9m at 2%	(180,000)
Total cost to you	**(240,000)**

There are some disadvantages to renting in that you may be forced to move every few years and you may not be able to decorate as you wish but often landlords will let you do anything that improves their property. If you dislike the turmoil of moving, go on holiday for a week and let professional removalists do it for you.

I recently found an unrenovated $7–$8m property in Point Piper, Sydney where they wanted $3,000 per week (2%). I offered them $2,000 per week (1.35%) plus I would renovate two bathrooms and paint and carpet it throughout. I knew I could renovate at wholesale prices and do it to my liking and still save money. They ended up renovating themselves, it's been vacant for six months and it's now down to $2,800 per week.

Renting may not be for you, but if you can follow the mindset shift, it might get you to think differently in other parts of your strategy.

The end game

Before you get into any investment you need to know your exit strategy. Ultimately if the assets are solid and continue to rise, why would you ever sell?

My initial aim was to build a $10m portfolio as I estimated that it should then rise by $500k–$1m pa on average. If I was $8m (80% LVR) in debt, there would be enough capital growth for me to cover the difference between the rent and the mortgage, have enough buffer to cover the lean times and enough money to live off. My debt would continue to rise but my assets should rise by even more.

If property prices continue to double roughly every seven years, the initial difference between the rent (4%) and the mortgage (8%) would be $240k and if I needed $160k cash to live off, the figures would look something like this:

Year 0	Year 7	Year 14	Year 21
10	20	40	80
(8)	(10)	(11)	(11)
2	**10**	**29**	**69**

By Year 8 it should become positive cash flow. By Year 11 it would create $320k income before tax and so my debt would level off.

Why you should still never sell

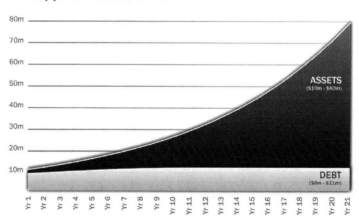

Loans taken for personal income wouldn't be tax deductible and I am assuming I am no longer working and don't get any tax rebates on the mortgage loss anyway.

If you are concerned about being in debt and susceptible to interest rate rises then you could either fix all of your loans for 10 years (the rates are not too dissimilar to the variable rates) or you could simply cash in some of your portfolio, pay the capital gains tax and reinvest in something safe. I personally think that property is the safest thing to invest in and if you invest in anything else you are likely to pay tax on the income it produces, meaning that you would need to earn $280k to be left with a net $140k.

REALITY CHECK

Do you believe that the notion that 'debt is a bad thing' is a concept that has been passed down from previous generations?

☐ Yes ☐ No

Do you sense that many people tend to see the potential of property investment only in retrospect ('if only we'd bought that place years ago...')?

☐ Yes ☐ No

Do you see the need for an opinion on the value of a property other than the real estate agent's assessment?

☐ Yes ☐ No

Do you believe your attitude to investment will change as your life circumstances change?

☐ Yes ☐ No

If you've answered 'yes' to any of these questions, keep reading.

6

The best way to make money is to spend money – wisely

Rather than trying to get rich from saving money,
you need to spend money to make money

My parents' generation were taught to do every task themselves – why pay someone else when you can do it yourself? We're smarter-thinking now, and if we earn $100 an hour in our profession and we pay our cleaner $25 an hour, it makes more sense for us to spend an extra hour at work and pay the cleaner for four hours' work.

Manage a team

If you are a busy high income earner who wishes to invest in property it is imperative to learn the value of outsourcing to experts in their field. There's no point learning how to do your own conveyancing if it's simply a matter of paying someone else $1,500 for the one or two times a year you might buy property. In your current role you probably manage a team of staff with unique skills to run your business or division, and as a property investor you need to do the same.

If you are going to outsource, you need to ensure that you go to specialists who are property investors in their own right, otherwise they may not understand the big picture of what you're trying to achieve.

If you ask a typical accountant if you should you pay off your home loan most of them would say, 'yes, you should pay it off because it's bad debt – and it's not tax deductible as it's on your own home'. But as an entrepreneur and property investor I'd rather concentrate on using my equity to buy another property that makes me an extra $100k pa rather than save a few thousand in tax. Sometimes accountants are so focused on saving tax they can't see the bigger picture. And being a reformed accountant, I should know.

Many people are not keen on paying for pre-purchase inspections (building inspectors, valuers, strata inspectors) as there's no guarantee that they will be successful at auction so they perceive it to be wasted money. However the chances are that if you know the market well enough you will buy within one or two auctions. Even if you spend $3,000–$4,000 rather than $1,000 on inspections it's well worth the investment as you could make a $50k–100k error by overpaying, not seeing a major structural problem or not realising that special levies are soon due. Even multiple inspections cost less than 1% of your proposed purchase. If you're investing $1m you'd be silly not to get professional advice.

If something goes wrong and the property isn't worth what was stated, you can possibly sue the valuer. Or if the building falls down the next day, you can sue the building inspector. You certainly don't want to build an investment portfolio based on suing people, but you need to have safeguards in place. You've still got to be responsible for your decision, but at least if you pay professionals to do the job, you are dealing with people who carry indemnity insurance.

Build a professional team of advisers

If you're going to build a property portfolio you'll need a professional team of advisers as you won't have the time or expertise to do it yourself. A professional is almost guaranteed to do it better than you.

The people you need are as follows:

Accountant

Before you buy your first property you'll need an accountant to check your figures. They can calculate a sensitivity analysis to ensure that your investing strategy will work no matter what happens in the economy and they can also calculate how much cash you may need to hold your portfolio in the short term.

Many property investors purchase under a company and/or trust structure because it gives asset protection and more flexibility to move profits and losses between partners.

Unless your accountant is a property investor they really won't understand the intricacies of what you are trying to achieve. You want an accountant who can educate you, not the other way around.

It costs a few thousand dollars to set up a company and trust structure which is a small price when you consider a $1m property doubling to $2 million in 7–10 years will produce a $1m capital gain. Any tax savings will more than outweigh the small setup costs.

Solicitor

You also need a good solicitor. Although it is cheaper to use a conveyancer, it's worth paying the extra to have a more broadly qualified legal adviser who can foresee some wider issues. This especially applies if you're buying off-the-plan properties, trying to undergo major refurbishment or strata titling a block of units. The extra $500 you might pay a solicitor could save you $50k down the track.

It's not worth doing it yourself – what if the laws have recently changed? What if the strata is more complicated that expected? What if you make a mistake? Your time is better spent dealing with your own business

A typical solicitor will charge $1,000–$2,000 for a straightforward property purchase.

Independent valuer

My number one tip in investing is to always use an independent valuer every time you purchase a property. You need someone who is not emotionally tied to the investment, who will provide an independent professional opinion of what that property is worth. It might cost $500–$600 (on a $1m property) but can easily save you $100k from an emotional overpayment. You might also be able to use this information in your property negotiations.

Independent is the key word. You don't want to rely on your real estate agent's valuer because they will almost certainly send you to one of their contacts who may provide a generous valuation because they want the agent to give them more valuations in the future.

I never negotiate lower fees with valuers. I want to be their most important and well paying client as that should ensure they spend the appropriate time preparing my report and gathering as many comparisons of similar properties that have sold to give me the most accurate valuation. If they work for a reduced fee their work may become sloppy which might result in me overpaying for a property.

Building inspector

You will also need a building inspector to make sure that the construction is sound. Even if it's a strata block and it's the strata's responsibility to fix up any issues, you need to foresee any future costs as you'll still be paying your share anyway.

For example, one of my properties required a $50k per unit expenditure to render the building, fix the roof, guttering and a whole number of other issues. While that's money well spent – because it will probably increase the property's value by $100k–$150k I needed to know that I was facing this sort of expenditure in advance so I could work out my cash flow.

With a house purchase it's definitely worth using a building inspector as there are a lot of subsidiary issues that can arise, and they may be able to do the pest inspection at the same time.

A building inspection may cost $400–$500 but if that inspector reports that the property needs $10k–$20k spent on it soon, it's well worth buying that information.

Property manager

You'll also need a property manager. Some people boast that they have saved $1,200 a year by managing the property themselves because it's easy to manage – and yes it can be. But if you've got 5–10 properties you won't want a phone call at midnight about a broken toilet or some other $50–$100 decision that you're going to have to agree to anyway! What's the point of you leaving your well paid job or having your leisure time disrupted to deal with a mundane problem?

When you're investing in property at a young age, money is tight and you may not be able to afford a property manager. But if you're a high income earner and you're building a reasonable portfolio, you'll need to delegate because you've surely got better things to do with your time.

A good property manager is in the market 24/7 and has a better idea of what rents are achievable so they are more likely to get you a higher rent when the market changes. They are more used to scrutinising tenant applications and not putting up with lame excuses for the rent not being paid.

Many property investors have sold profitable properties only because they are fed up with dealing with tenants. Why sell an investment that makes you $100k p.a. when you can get rid of any tenant hassles for just over $2,000 a year?

Buyer's agent

Buyer's agents are the opposite to real estate agents (selling agents) in that they work for you, the buyer, rather than the seller. If the seller is hiring a professional to negotiate their side of the sale, as an amateur why wouldn't you hire a professional to negotiate for you too?

Buyer's agents typically charge around 2–3% of a property's value to search, negotiate and purchase it for you and to manage that process. They will bid at auction or try to buy it prior to the listed sale date. So why pay $20–30k for them to buy a $1m property when you could do it yourself?

Here's why:

They do it every day

Buyer's agents are in the market all day every day and so there's a very good chance that they're going to do it better than someone who only does it occasionally.

They've got insider knowledge

Many properties that get sold don't even go on the open market as many owners don't want the hassle of a series of open houses, prefer to be private or are simply in a rush to sell. As buyer's agents are constantly in contact with real estate agents and are buying multiple properties, they get to hear of properties for sale before the average mum and dad.

Agents often prefer dealing with them

When agents deal with the average buyer they often get messed around, misled, toyed with and let down at the last minute. The average property buyers are unsure of what they are doing and are therefore indecisive. Buyer's agents who perhaps purchase one property per week tend to be more efficient with their decisions and actions. Emotional buyers may well pay more for a property but often the selling agent would prefer to get a guaranteed sale for less money rather than a sale that may fall over.

With a real estate agent's commission structure it doesn't really make a difference whether they sell for $1m or $1.05m. If a buyer's agent can buy a property without the agent having to open up the property repeatedly that's probably 20 hours of their time that is now freed up to try to secure the next listing. Better to get two $20k commissions rather than one $22k one.

They make factual decisions, not emotional ones

Buyer's agents are being paid to find you a good investment and that means they have to consider all aspects of the property and the price. This leads them to make factual financial decisions rather than the emotional ones that most other buyers make, especially when choosing their own homes.

They have the time

If you have to inspect 50–100 properties to understand the market and find the right one, do you really have the time to do it yourself? Viewing five to 10 properties each Saturday would mean 3–6 months of lost weekends for each property you want to buy. Most people get fed up and buy the next thing they see at any price which is no way to build a stable property portfolio. Buyer's agents will be out there every week no matter if they buy or not so there's less chance of them making a pressured decision.

If you're paid $100–$200/hr at work your limited leisure time should be worth at least $500–$1,000 an hour. If a buyer's agent is also going to get you a better property at a cheaper price, learn to spend $1 to make $2. If a buyer's agent can save you $100k on the property, it's worth paying the $20k–$30k. Even if they don't buy you a cheap property but instead find a property that's going to grow at 10% a year rather than 8%, you'll be making $20k a year extra for the rest of your life.

REALITY CHECK

Do you have a house cleaner, window cleaner or gardener, ? Do you take your ironing to the laundrette? Do you regard this as money well spent?

⬔ Yes ⬔ No

Given that they're supposed to be experts in financial principles, have you ever wondered why many accountants seem to live quite modestly?

⬔ Yes ⬔ No

Would you agree that with everything else going on in your life, the time you'd have available to manage a property portfolio is very limited?

⬔ Yes ⬔ No

Any more 'yes' answers? Keep reading, just two short chapters to go.

7

The cost of doing nothing could be the biggest cost of all

If you can afford to buy, buy now

The cost of putting off your decision can be very high. You may have thought of investing in property for a long time but one year leads to another and suddenly you may find you haven't done it.

The property market is constantly changing just like any other market and there is no guarantee that it will rise in the short term. Therefore a lot of prospective buyers say, 'I'll leave it till next year when the market's moving'. But generally, the long term trend is always clear and residential property generally goes up in value.

No matter how much of an expert you think you are, you can't foresee the top or the bottom of the market. No one rings a bell when it's bottomed. So the general rule is – if you can afford to buy, *buy now* – because on average if you buy at a reasonable price, you'll make money over the long term. Whereas if you keep questioning it and wait for the market to go up, by the time you get the right signals the market will have already started to move and you will already be paying too much for the property. Every year there's a different issue that could test your resolve: the Olympic Games, housing affordability, the US sub-prime crisis, interest rates, etc, etc.

Even a 12-month delay can make a huge difference to where you are in 10–20 years time because if property rises at 10% a year, a $1m property is rising on average by $2,000 a week. So each week you delay the decision that's $2,000 per property. So if you could buy five properties right now that's $10,000 you're missing out on with every passing week.

Also if you get into the market now rather than in seven years time, and say you've got 21 years until you retire:

- *a $1m property will go up in value to $2 million in seven years*

- *$4 million in 14 years*

- *$8 million in 21 years.*

But if you delay your decision and you've only got 14 years rather than 21 you're not missing out on $1m growing to $2 million, you're actually missing out on $4 million growing to $8 million because having that extra seven years makes the difference between $4 million and $8 million – so you're losing out on $4 million per property.

Years	0	7	14	21
Do it now	$1m	$2m	$4m	$8m
Procrastinate		$1m	$2m	$4m

Also you may be paying a lot of tax now, so the sooner you invest, the sooner you get your tax deductions and reduce your tax. And that means you can move on quicker and quicker. The sooner you do it, the sooner you can get into your next property and the next one after that. So you don't just buy a property and hold onto it forever, quite often you refinance every year and you use that money to either boost your buffer or to buy more properties.

Most people don't invest in property using this strategy mainly because they just don't know about it. Most people are too scared of debt to bother doing the maths. But using an expert can show you what you need to do. You don't necessarily have to do it yourself. If you understand the numbers you can get over your fear of debt – and there are plenty of examples of successful people who can prove that debt is actually a good thing. A good accountant will usually say 'investing in property is good' – you just need to speak to the right accountant who understands the complete picture.

The main way to become successful at investing is you need to have a reason to go out there and do it. What is it that you're really trying to achieve and what's going to happen if you don't achieve that?

Say you have a $2 million house and you buy a $1m investment unit (and you get it valued so you *know* it's worth $1m) even if you sold it next day you'd probably get at least $900k. So you'd probably be only losing $100k at the most, which on a $2 million portfolio is not a big risk.

If you bought that first property well and did buy it under value, or alternatively you bought a good property and then waited a year, chances are you've probably made $100k already. So even if you sold it quickly you'd probably get your money back anyway.

Making the first step into investing isn't necessarily a big risk especially if you've already got equity and money behind you. But until you try it you're never going to know.

With all the thousands of people I've spoken to at seminars, from teaching people, getting feedback from my books and hosting over 250 shows on Sky News Business, I have learned that most people hold the same issues in common. So if you're worried about debt or you're not too sure about the strategies, don't fear because it's something that can be solved with the right advice and if you start slowly, you'll build that confidence over time.

Any money you pay for professionals is an investment for yourself. If you're a high income and time-poor executive and there's no chance of you doing it yourself, pay someone to do it for you. When you want a share portfolio you're happy to pay investment advisers 1% to look after it for you. Effectively that's what I'm proposing you should do with property – *deal only with experts* because the experts who are doing it every day have the expertise.

Don't die wondering! Have a go. A chance to enjoy your retirement years financially free – who said retirement has to start at 65? I've been enjoying it since my 30s!

REALITY CHECK

Have you ever felt a palpable sense of relief after completing a job – say, getting insurance – that you've been putting off again and again?

☐ Yes ☐ No

With the benefit of hindsight, would you have pursued a property investment strategy at a younger age?

☐ Yes ☐ No

Was that a couple more 'yes' answers? Just one more chapter, where I show you how to put everything I've said into action.

8
How to get started on your own empire – effortlessly

Many people aim to build a property portfolio but few ever achieve it. Here's the guaranteed and simple way.

When I worked at Deloitte, my colleagues couldn't understand how I could afford to drive expensive cars and live in gorgeous beachside properties. They earned more than I did so why did I have the luxuries that they didn't?

At 31 I began teaching other people the secret to leveraging your time and money to build wealth through property. Over the next six years I found that while most people are keen to increase their wealth the majority of them fail to follow all the necessary steps and they end up doing nothing.

So I decided to do it for them. And I can do it for you too.

Through my business *Your Empire* I now assist time-poor professionals to build property portfolios exactly the same as I have done for myself. While *Your Empire* charges a fee for doing so, the profits they make far outweigh the costs.

If you would like *Your Empire* to build a property portfolio for you, here's briefly what you can expect. There are four parts to the service – **Engage, Locate, Negotiate, Renovate.**

1. Engage

I know you are time-poor, so this is really the only stage where you need to be actively involved. After this point, we take care of everything else and your involvement can be limited to phone and email, if that's all you require. You can of course remain more involved if you wish. At the Engagement Stage we discuss your investment and lifestyle goals to determine the type of Personal Property Portfolio Strategy that's right for you. We also need to line up the third parties who will be involved in the buying process: financier, accountant, lawyer, valuer and inspectors. *Your Empire* can introduce you to experts in each of these fields unless you have existing contacts you prefer to use. Either way is fine with us.

At the end of the Engagement Stage you should have:

- *your Personal Property Portfolio strategy, which can then be checked by your accountant and/or financial planner*

- *finance approval, from your chosen bank or mortgage broker*

- *your solicitor arranged for contract reviews*

- *a valuer for independent confirmation of your property value*

- *a building and strata inspector.*

2. Locate

Obviously some properties make better investments than others. It's about getting the right price on the right property, not just the lowest absolute price. It's also about knowing that the investment value and rent potential are there to give you both cash flow and capital growth.

To locate the right property, *Your Empire* puts a team of industry professionals at your disposal. We are in the property market 24/7, constantly reviewing investment opportunities for our clients. We have access to the latest demographic trends and property price movements in your selected location areas and we are skilled in interpreting this data correctly. We review the market at both macro and micro level.

A large number of properties that come on the market are never advertised to the public as the sellers require a quick sale and/or do not want the expense and inconvenience of going through a lengthy auction process. Real estate agents often prefer dealing directly with companies such as *Your Empire* as they know that we represent serious buyers who can make a quick decision for the right opportunity. When we find potential properties for you, you are welcome to view them yourself, or remain dispassionate and let *Your Empire* make an objective decision on a prospective property, with your inspectors backing up that decision.

During the Locate stage *Your Empire* will give you:

- *regular summaries of properties that fit your buying profile*

- *regular phone sessions to evaluate current options.*

3. Negotiate

You'd be surprised how much room to negotiate there is in property investment. If you do it firmly but fairly you can get a great outcome. *Your Empire* will negotiate several buying factors on your behalf, price being just one of them.

In many cases we are able to secure a property prior to auction because the vendors can be assured we have a client standing by with finance approved, so there will be no long drawn-out settlement.

The most important factor in negotiation, though, is that we are aiming to secure the right property for your strategy. It isn't worth squeezing a seller to secure the absolute best deal if in doing so we run the risk of losing the property. For the right property, the potential upside gain will outweigh any small concession in price.

Tenanting and ongoing property management

Your Empire will find the most suitable property manager for your property area. As several *Your Empire* clients may be using the same manager, we are able to negotiate favourable terms. They will be keen to ensure your property is well tenanted straight away at the highest possible rent. We will also help you gain fast access to the property to prepare it for new tenants.

During the negotiation stage *Your Empire* will:

- *negotiate the property purchase either before, during or after auction*

- *confirm with your mortgage broker, solicitor and other advisers that everything is in place for settlement*

- *help to secure a tenant for the property.*

4. Renovate

There are few properties sold that wouldn't benefit from some careful renovation. Doing the right work in the right way will add value to your investment and increase its rentable potential at the same time. Obviously it's a good idea to renovate before you tenant the property as the right type of works can create a substantial uplift on the rental value. As with property selection and purchase, renovation requires a detached view to make the right decisions. After all, it's unlikely you'll be living in this property yourself.

As *Your Empire* commissions millions of dollars of renovation work per year, we have competitively priced access to skilled, licensed tradespeople. We can line up each trade to come in as soon as the previous work is finished – if you've renovated before you'll know one of the main drags in time is waiting for tradesmen to start rather than to finish. In fact our tradespeople will guarantee to finish on time or they'll pay you the lost rent. They will also warrant any work they do for 12 months.

At the Renovate stage *Your Empire* will:

- *make recommendations for the works to be done*

- *discuss the pros and cons of different options and the likely returns*

- *introduce our network of licensed builders and tradesmen*

- *arrange estimates for various renovation works*

- *get interior designers to co-ordinate style and colour themes*

- *be on site to approve entry for trades and deliveries.*

The following pages are examples of properties we have bought. All of the properties were bought for long term growth. The market is constantly changing and so are individual suburbs so please contact us to discuss what is happening now.

REALITY CHECK

I now have two final questions for you:

☐ Are you ready?

☐ If not now, when?

Case studies

Buy and hold

VIEW FROM BALCONY

Purchase

- *Good condition two bedroom unit with lock up garage*
- *5 minutes walk to the beach*
- *Two large double bedrooms, both with built-in wardrobes*
- *Sunny balcony*
- *Clean and modern kitchen and bathroom*

Financials (est. 2015)

Cost	$900k
Rent	$750/wk
Rent %	4.3%

This property is in a very quiet street close to the beach.

If this high capital growth suburb rises at 7-10% per year the owner will make $63-90k+/yr.

Renovator's delight

Purchase

- Unrenovated two bedroom unit with lock up garage

- 5 minutes walk to two beaches

- North facing lounge, balcony and main bedroom

Improvements

- New polyurethane kitchen and bathroom

- Made an opening in the wall between kitchen and lounge

- New blinds, carpets, built-ins, cupboards, washer, dryer

Financials (est. 2015)

Cost	$850k
Renovation	$75k
Total cost	$925k
Valuation after	$950-975k
Profit	**$25-50k**

	Before	After
Valuation	$850k	**$950k**
Rent	$650/wk	**$800/wk**
Rent %	4%	**4.4%**

The project took six weeks to complete and the owner was completely passive during the process. If the $100-125k increase in value can be refinanced at 80% to give you $80k which pays for the $75k renovation and gives you up to an additional $5k-30k cash buffer. If this high capital growth suburb rises at 7-10% per year, the owner will make $67–98k per year.

Off the plan

Purchase

- One bedroom + study + courtyard garden

- Security undercover parking

- 500 metres walk to the beach

- Brand new apartment block of 30 units

- Due for completion 18 months from purchase

Financials (2008)

Cost	$485k
Expected value	$550k-$600k
Rent %	5%
Expected profit	**$50k-100k**
Deposit bond cost	$3k

This was an exclusive off the plan development that was a few hundred metres from the beach. A very rare opportunity to get into as there are not many new developments in the area. All of the properties were sold to family, friends and close contacts of the sales agent and so nothing was advertised to the public. I bought two properties for myself and four for my clients, negotiating over $10k per property off the already cheap price for buying in bulk.

Rather than put down a cash deposit I took out a deposit bond at a cost of $3k which guarantees the vendor I will come up with the funds on settlement. The expected profit is likely to be over $50k-100k.

Added bonus: if the property is valued at $600k on completion and I obtain 80% finance, the bank will be lending me $480k of the $485k purchase price which means I secure a $600k property for only $5k deposit and make $100k immediately.

Off the plan investments can be very speculative though and no one knows what the market will be like in the future.

Purchase

- *Unrenovated block of 5 x two bedroom units, 3 with ocean views*

- *Two lock-up garages*

- *5–10 minute walk to beach and shops*

- *Sydney's eastern suburbs*

- *Unused communal garden and tatty balcony over garage*

- *Single title building*

- *Cost $1.9m*

Making a million

Improvements

- Stripped all of the units and put in new kitchens, bathrooms, blinds, built-ins

- Converted two of the two bedroom units to three bedroom units

- Split up communal areas so each unit has a separate garden or large balcony

- Applied for a development application to add balconies to front of building

- Applied to council to strata title the block as five individual units

- Rendered the outside of the building, renewed paths and landscaped gardens

- Received 10 weeks access to renovate before settlement for a cost of $3k

Financials (2008)

Cost	$1.9m
Renovation	$600k
Total cost	$2.5m
Bank valuation	$3.5m
Profit	**$1m**

Added bonus: When the block is strata titled the property's value should rise by 10% to $3.8m. Refinancing to 80% would provide $3m which means that every cent that was put in to the property can be taken back out. You then own a $3.8m property with none of your own money in it. If this high capital growth suburb rises at 10% per year the owner will make $300k–$400k per year.

For more information on creating your empire effortlessly, please visit yourempire.com.au or contact us directly:

- t: 02 9994 8944
- e: info@yourempire.com.au
- office: Level 14, 309 Kent St, Sydney NSW 2000
- mail: PO Box N64, Grosvenor Place PO NSW 1220

Your Empire can help you buy and renovate homes and investment properties in all capital cities around Australia.

Made in United States
Orlando, FL
14 October 2023

37874437R00067